Cornerstones of Freedom

The Story of
THE BATTLE
OF BULL RUN

By Zachary Kent

Illustrated by David J. Catrow III

 CHILDRENS PRESS ®
CHICAGO

Library of Congress Cataloging-in-Publication Data

Kent, Zachary.
    The story of the Battle of Bull Run.

    (Cornerstones of freedom)
    Summary: Presents the events in the Civil War
leading up to the first major battle, at Bull Run in
1861, and describes that clash and its aftermath.
    1. Bull Run, 1st Battle, 1861 — Juvenile literature.
[1. Bull Run, 1st Battle, 1861. 2. United States —
History — Civil War, 1861-1865 — Campaigns] I. Catrow,
David J., ill. II. Title. III. Series.
E472.18.K46 1986   973.7'31   86-9642
ISBN 0-516-04703-5

All day long on Monday, July 22, 1861, soldiers streamed over the Potomac River bridges. Through a pouring rain they plodded, baffled and frightened, back to the safety of Washington, D.C. Along Pennsylvania Avenue they milled about in confused mobs of straggling companies, their once bright militia uniforms smoke stained, muddy, and sopping wet. Their stomachs growled with hunger while they stopped to rub the aching blisters on their feet. The poet Walt Whitman was present and wrote, "They drop down anywhere, on steps of houses, up close by the basements or fences, on the sidewalk, aside on some vacant lot, and deeply sleep.... Some clutch their muskets firmly.... Some in squads, comrades, brothers, close together—and on them, as they lay, sulkily drips the rain."

Thus the defeated Union army returned from the first major battle of the American Civil War. The capital city would never be the same, and neither would the Virginia battlefield twenty miles away, the fields and woods along the winding stream called Bull Run. One Federal officer explained to a reporter, "We're all coming out of Virginny as far as we can and pretty well whipped, too. . . . I'm going home. I've had enough of fighting to last my lifetime." Many others felt the same. What had happened at Bull Run made another Union soldier exclaim, "I can truly say that I have seen all the horrors of war."

The United States was gripped in a struggle that was tearing the country in two. For more than forty years arguments had raged over the issue of slavery. In the North, where factories abounded, thousands of European immigrants were willing to work for low wages. Most Northerners had no use for slavery and many considered it to be cruel and immoral. The South, however, depended upon slavery for the success of its farming economy.

As new lands west of the Mississippi River opened, Southerners demanded that slavery be allowed there, too. Northerners resisted the exten-

sion of slavery. In the Kansas Territory, bands of proslavery ruffians fought a guerrilla war against antislavery settlers.

The final crisis arrived with Abraham Lincoln's election as sixteenth president of the United States in November 1860. Lincoln, a Northerner from Illinois, had once stated, "A house divided against itself cannot stand. I believe this government cannot endure permanently half slave and half free." Many angry Southerners feared Lincoln would abolish slavery. They insisted the federal government had no right to force laws upon the separate states. On December 20, 1860, rather than submit, the state of South Carolina left the Union. Florida, Georgia, Alabama, Mississippi, Louisiana, and Texas soon followed. Together these seceded states formed the Confederate States of America with Jefferson Davis as their president.

At his inauguration on March 4, 1861, President Lincoln warned the South, "In your hands, my dissatisfied countrymen, and not in mine, is the momentous issue of civil war." He promised not to attack the South unless it first began the conflict.

The Southerners would not listen. In April, Confederate cannon fired on Fort Sumter in the harbor of Charleston, South Carolina, forcing the withdrawal of the Union garrison. The next day Lincoln called for 75,000 troops to put down the rebellion. Unwilling to fight their sister slaveholding states, Virginia, North Carolina, Arkansas, and Tennessee soon also quit the Union.

Now that the war had begun, the people of Washington felt nervous. Only the Potomac River separated that city from the enemy in Virginia.

With lightning speed, state militias gathered and hastened southward to save the capital. Dressed in handsome uniforms, carrying new guns and equipment, these innocent men and boys were more than eager to fight. At one railroad station in Maine, Colonel Oliver Howard overheard his proud soldiers express their confidence.

"Oh, pshaw, father! Don't be gloomy; I shan't be gone more'n two months."

"Come, mother, don't be alarmed; this will be a short trip."

"Hurrah, hurrah! We'll make short work of this business; only let's be off."

Across the North, from Maine to Minnesota, similar farewells were being taken. It was no different in the South, where the rush to join the Confederate army took on a circus atmosphere. Explained George A. Gibbs, a Mississippi boy, "Nothing would do me but to enlist. My parents pleaded with me, saying I was too young to go to war. . . . But nothing could shake my resolution to be a soldier." Many Southerners wanted to get into the fight before all the "fun" was over.

By early July enough Union soldiers had arrived in Washington to protect the city. They marched in review before the president and set up a ring of

camps around the district. Militiaman Augustus Woodbury wrote home, "You can go up into the dome of the Capitol and see tents of the Federal army in every direction as far as you can see."

The Confederate government chose Richmond, Virginia, for its capital. Horace Greeley, the editor of the *New York Tribune,* demanded, "Forward to Richmond! Forward to Richmond! The Rebel Congress must not be allowed to meet there on the twentieth of July!"

Throughout the North came a call for immediate action. Feeling the tremendous public pressure, Lincoln ordered an advance.

Under the command of Brigadier General Irvin McDowell, the inexperienced Union soldiers were quickly formed into companies, regiments, brigades, and huge divisions. On July 16, an army of 35,000 Federals set out on a march into Virginia. Mile after mile the long column tramped forward. As yet, the army had no standard uniform. Many of the regiments wore blue, while others preferred gray. (Later, the Union soldiers all wore blue and the Confederates wore gray.) Some were dressed in kilts like Scottish Highlanders and some wore the baggy trousers of French Zouaves.

These men were so high-spirited at the start of this great adventure that they often were beyond control. Passing farmyards, they shot at pigs and chased after chickens. They broke into houses and carried away such useless items as a feather bed, a sledgehammer, and a huge looking glass. "They stopped every moment to pick blackberries," complained General McDowell. At every creek and well the hot and dusty men broke ranks to fill their canteens. All these interruptions made progress slow, but it was a grand march all the same.

McDowell led his carefree army twenty miles southwest toward the railroad junction at Manassas. For months Southern troops had gathered there under the command of Pierre G.T. Beauregard, the very general who had forced the surrender of Fort Sumter. A handsome, dashing figure, Beauregard had graduated second out of forty-five cadets at West Point in 1838, while his classmate, Irvin McDowell, finished twenty-third.

Beauregard understood that the defense of all northern Virginia depended on Manassas. He ordered his army of twenty thousand men to take up a position just north of the town. A crooked stream some thirty feet wide offered the best military advantage. It was called Bull Run, and its banks were high and its water deep. With his men dug in along the river's fords and its one bridge, Beauregard awaited the approach of the Northern enemy.

For his headquarters, the Southern general chose the farmhouse of a Mr. Wilmer McLean. On the afternoon of July 18, Beauregard and his staff sat down to dinner when a sudden booming of cannon fire shook them in their seats. As the officers stared at each other, one stray shell crashed through the

chimney and exploded in the fireplace. The Federals
had arrived at last and were beginning the attack.

Just north of Bull Run, a division of Union men,
led by crusty General Daniel Tyler, tried to force a
crossing at Blackburn's Ford. The rebels met the
attack, and Tyler's men soon discovered how tough a
war could be. Musket balls whistled through the air

like hailstones. Pushing his brigade forward, Colonel William T. Sherman was shocked. "For the first time in my life I saw cannonballs strike men and crash through the trees and saplings above and around us." Having found the center of the Confederate line, McDowell ordered his soldiers to pull back.

While the Union general spent the next two days scouting for a better place to cross Bull Run, General Beauregard begged for reinforcements to bolster his outnumbered army. In the Shenandoah Valley, sixty miles to the west, Confederate General Joseph Johnston commanded some eleven thousand men. Johnston received orders to slip away from the enemy in his front and bring his army by train to Manassas. "General Beauregard is attacked," Johnston shouted to his troops. "Every moment now is precious." In answer his men raised their hats and cheered with wild enthusiasm.

Into the night of July 20 the trains rolled to Manassas with whistles blowing. Lines of wagons hauled supplies of food and ammunition to the front. As Johnston's brigades joined Beauregard's Confederates along the marshy banks of Bull Run, they sensed the coming of a great battle.

In the Union camps also, the soldiers felt nervous and excited. Few of them could sleep. Around the twinkling campfires they wrote final letters home and told boastful stories. One New York private wrote, "Not a thought of defeat or reverse of any kind entered our minds. We had only to go forth and conquer."

General McDowell finally had a plan of action. By swinging half his army several miles north across Bull Run at the Sudley Springs Ford, he hoped to attack Beauregard's unprotected left flank. At the same time Tyler's division was to push down the Warrenton Turnpike and threaten the Confederates at the only bridge, called the Stone Bridge. In the early morning of July 21 Tyler's men started across the fields. In the darkness Ohio soldier George M. Finch complained, "We never knew where a fence or a tree was located . . . until we ran slap against it."

With only eleven hundred men defending the Stone Bridge, the Confederates were in serious danger. Luckily these soldiers were commanded by Colonel Nathan "Shanks" Evans. Called "Shanks" because of his bowlegs, Evans was a tough, whiskey-drinking soldier who loved to fight.

At dawn, the thunder of Tyler's artillery burst through the trees and over the Stone Bridge, but Colonel Evans wisely sensed the main attack would soon come from Sudley Springs. Shifting most of his forces, he rushed troops to the left, up Matthews Hill. The men fell into line just in time to meet the first of McDowell's divisions. At 9:30 A.M., the battle began in earnest.

Already exhausted from their night march, troops
from Rhode Island, New Hampshire, and New York
stormed forward, one regiment after another, at the
direction of Colonel Ambrose Burnside. Never
before under fire, these soldiers were fascinated by
the snapping sound of the bullets in the leaves.

Though faced by an overwhelming force,
"Shanks" Evans ordered an attack of his own. Leading the desperate charge were five hundred Louis-
ianans commanded by giant, 275-pound Major
Roberdeau Wheat. "Wheat's Tigers" growled and
yelled as they ran forward, waving their shining
bowie knives. For a time they kept the Federals off

balance. In the middle of this fierce fight a bullet entered one of Major Wheat's armpits, passed through his chest, and came out the other side. His men lugged his heavy body behind the battle lines. The doctors who saw the wound said it would surely kill him. "I don't feel like dying yet," the major angrily grumbled. Defying the odds, Wheat would survive to fight in other battles.

Aware now of his army's danger, Beauregard ordered Barnard Bee's brigade and Colonel Francis Bartow's Seventh and Eighth Georgia Regiments to Matthews Hill. At the hill's summit, "we halted," remembered M.J. Solomons, "breathless, footsore, and exhausted, but eager for the fray." Another Georgian had different memories. "I felt that I was in the presence of death," he recalled. "My first thought was, 'This is unfair; somebody is to blame for getting us all killed.'"

Across open fields these men lunged through smoke toward the enemy. One soldier who survived remembered, "The balls just poured on us, struck our muskets and hats and bodies." Private Dunwoody Jones, while charging, felt something strike his foot. Stopping in the middle of the fight, he calmly took off his shoe and pried a bullet out of the heel.

By 11:00 it was obvious the Southern soldiers could not hold off the strong Union advance. With his men already falling back, General Bee ordered a retreat. In confusion the Southerners ran down Matthews Hill, across the Warrenton Turnpike, and started up a second great rise called Henry Hill. Watching from a distance, General McDowell beamed with pleasure. "Victory! Victory! The day is ours," he shouted, riding his horse among his Union troops.

To stop the Union men on Henry Hill there stood only Hampton's Legion of six hundred fresh South Carolina troops. These men, commanded by wealthy planter Colonel Wade Hampton, fought a brave holding action, while around them their bloodied and frightened comrades hurried to the rear. During this fight Confederate Private James Lowndes saw a puff of smoke from an enemy cannon on Matthews Hill. "I kept my eye in that direction, and in a few seconds saw the ball coming exactly where I was standing." He stepped aside just in time and the spinning cannonball crashed into the ranks, killing several of his comrades.

Hampton's hard-pressed men soon retreated, joining the growing crowd of beaten Confederates. To their left, at the very brow of the hill, some saw the arrival of General Thomas Jackson and his Virginia brigade. Out of the dust and turmoil, General Bee rode up to him.

"General, they are beating us back," he cried.

"Sir, we will give them the bayonet," calmly answered Jackson.

Back into the smoke Bee galloped until he reached a tangle of his men. Rising in his stirrups, he pointed his sword. "Look," he shouted. "There is Jackson standing like a stone wall! Rally behind the Virginians!" Some of the men took heart. Confederates who had fought all morning tried to re-form on Jackson's solid new line. Within minutes, a bullet struck General Bee, knocking him from his horse with a deadly wound, but his stirring words had created a legend. From that moment forward, General Jackson was known as "Stonewall" Jackson.

The gunfire grew hotter as McDowell's Yankee regiments pushed across the Warrenton Turnpike and started up Henry Hill. To soften the Confederate line, McDowell ordered eleven cannon to the very edge of the hilltop, not far from a lone, two-story farmhouse. Determined to rid the place of suspected enemy sharpshooters, Captain James

Ricketts turned his guns upon the house and sent shell after shell into it. There were no soldiers inside, only poor old Mrs. Henry and a servant. Widow Henry lay sick in her upstairs bedroom when a shell smashed through the wall and knocked her from her bed. She died before the end of the day.

To support his batteries, McDowell sent forward the Eleventh New York "Fire Zouaves," a regiment composed mostly of New York City firemen. Dressed in baggy red trousers and trim blue vests, the Zouaves dropped their heavy knapsacks and rushed into the battle. "The dust under our feet," said Private Lewis Metcalf, "was thrown into the air and filled our eyes and mouths, and the fierce July sun blazed remorselessly upon us."

The ex-firemen dashed up the hill and across the Henry cornfield, only to meet General Jackson's line hidden in the woods nearby. The Confederates fired a fearful volley. The bullets, said Private Metcalf, came "crashing through the cornfield, singing and whistling around our ears, making the air blue and sulfurous with smoke." The shocked New Yorkers fell back, leaving the cannon unprotected.

At that very moment a body of men stepped out of the woods and toward the guns. This was the Thirty-third Virginia Regiment, whose uniforms happened to be blue. All day the mixed uniform colors between the armies had caused confusion, but never more gravely than now. Colonel Arthur Cummings marched his men to within seventy yards of the batteries. The Union gunners held their fire, unsure whether they faced friends or foes. In an instant the Virginians opened fire. Watching from a distance was Union Colonel William W. Averell. Later he wrote, "It seemed as though every man and horse of that battery just laid right down and died." The Virginians swarmed in triumph around the cannon as the surviving gunners fled.

Another piece of luck brought the Confederate cavalry at that moment charging into the flustered

Zouaves. Led by Lieutenant Colonel J.E.B. Stuart, the eager horsemen galloped into the ranks, slashing left and right with their sabers. One Confederate lieutenant named William Blackford leaned from his saddle and fired his carbine rifle into a man's stomach.

"I could not help feeling a little sorry for the fellow," he later admitted, "for the carbine blew a hole as big as my arm clear through him."

This deadly charge, together with the loss of the eleven cannon, destroyed much of the Federal spirit. All along the line it seemed the tide of the fight was slowly turning.

For the next two hours the raging battle seesawed back and forth. Colonel Hampton led a downhill charge and was stunned by a bullet that grazed his scalp. Union troops counterattacked and retook the lost cannon, only to give them up again. Tyler's division waded across Bull Run, and near the Robinson farm Colonel Sherman sent forward the kilted Seventy-ninth New York Regiment. "Come on, my brave Highlanders," shouted Colonel James Cameron, brother of the secretary of war. Two heavy volleys and Cameron and many of his brave men lay dying on the field.

Into the afternoon one Union regiment after another tried to break Stonewall Jackson's line on Henry Hill. A newspaperman on the scene scribbled that "for one long mile the whole valley is a boiling crater of dust and smoke." In this murky fog, amid whizzing bullets and shrieking horses, the Union troops became jumbled and frantic.

Behind the Confederate line, General Johnston met E. Kirby Smith's brigade, just then arrived on the Manassas trains. "Take them to the front," yelled Johnston. "Go where the fire is hottest." These and other reinforcements reached the field exactly when they were needed most. Their added strength proved too much for the Federals. The weary Northern soldiers suddenly broke and started for the rear at the sight of the fresh Confederate troops. Fearing capture, they threw away their rifles and equipment and hurried back across the Sudley Springs Ford and over the Stone Bridge. No officer's command could stop the panic that surged through the Union ranks. From Henry Hill, Confederate Lieutenant Blackford observed that suddenly "the whole field was a confused swarm of men, like bees, running away as fast as their legs could carry them."

To make matters worse, many ladies and gentle-men of fashionable society had come down from Washington that day to enjoy the battle. With picnic lunches at hand, they had expected to watch a Union victory from the safety of the hills north of Bull Run. Now, in horror, they were swept up in the retreat. Horses and carriages clogged the roads and scat-tered this way and that. Knapsacks, blankets, trunks, clothes, entire wagons of supplies, all were carelessly left behind. The combined rush of soldiers and civilians escaping along the Warrenton Turnpike sounded like "a hurricane at sea."

In the evening it began to rain, turning all the roads to mud. The Battle of Bull Run was over and its worst damage done. Through the woods and over the rolling fields lay the bodies of the dead—481 Union and 387 Confederate. The drizzle washed the grime from their faces as burial parties carried them to shallow graves.

More than 2,500 men remained moaning upon the battleground. In the night a Zouave, Private Metcalf, shot through the leg, called back and forth to wounded friends. In crude field hospitals, Confederate surgeons went at their bloody work, cutting off mangled arms and legs.

Still the Southerners were thrilled with their victory. They believed the war would soon be over. In the days to come people named racehorses, steamboats, and even babies in honor of General Beauregard. The success of the Confederates in the largest battle ever fought in North America sparked an explosion of joy throughout the South.

In Washington, clouds of gloom darkened the streets. McDowell's beaten men trudged through the rain. Officers searched through the crowds, trying to put together their broken regiments. Ambulance wagons brought in the wounded, and women served soup and bread to the hungry.

President Lincoln spent a sleepless night but awoke even more determined to continue the fight. From the shame of defeat the North quickly learned the hard realities of war. "I had a dim notion about the 'romance' of a soldier's life," confessed a Union soldier. "I have bravely got over it since." With a new sense of purpose the North immediately began to prepare tougher, better-trained armies. In other battles Union men would fight hard to avenge their fallen brothers.

In August 1862, the armies of the North and South clashed in another great battle near Manassas. Historians called it the Second Battle of Bull Run. Again soldiers trampled over the farm owned by Mr. Wilmer McLean. Afterward, in search of peace, McLean sold his property and moved away. But the armies eventually found him once more, in the country settlement of Appomattox Court House, in central Virginia. By chance, McLean's new house was chosen for the surrender of Confederate General Robert E. Lee to Union General Ulysses S. Grant on April 9, 1865. The war that started with a cannon shell in McLean's dining room beside Bull Run was destined to end with Lee's surrender in McLean's Appomattox living room.

About the Author

Zachary Kent grew up in Little Falls, New Jersey, and received an English degree from St. Lawrence University. Following college he worked at a New York City literary agency for two years and then launched his writing career. To support himself while writing, he has worked as a taxi driver, a shipping clerk, and a house painter. Mr Kent has had a lifelong interest in American history. Studying the U.S. presidents was his childhood hobby. His collection of presidential items includes books, pictures, and games, as well as several autographed letters.

About the Artist

David J. Catrow III was born in Virginia and grew up in Hudson, Ohio. He spent three years in the United States Navy as a hospital corpsman and subsequently attended Kent State University, where he majored in biology. He is a self-taught illustrator. Mr. Catrow currently lives in Springfield, Ohio with his wife Deborah Ann and children Hillary and D.J. He is an editorial cartoonist for the *Springfield New-Sun.* The artist would like to thank his wife Deborah for her constant support and inspiration.